SOUTH KOREA

Amazing & Interesting Facts You Didn't know Before

BANDANA OJHA

<u>Introduction</u>
Filled with up-to-date information, fascinating & fun facts this book **SOUTH KOREA: Amazing & Interesting Facts You Didn't Know Before**" is the best book for kids to find out more about "The land of morning calm" This book would satisfy the children's curiosity and help them to understand why South Korea attracts millions of visitors annually and what makes it different from other Asian Countries. This book gives a story, history & explores the country's best cuisine, architecture, fashion, art, language, people, places, national symbols, inventions, technology and many more. It is a fun and fascinating way for young readers to find out more interesting facts. This is a great chance for every kid to expand their knowledge about South Korea and impress family and friends with all "discovered and never knew before" amazing facts.

South Korea, officially the Republic of Korea (ROK), is a country in East Asia.

It is the southern part of the Korean Peninsula and sharing a land border with North Korea.

Its western border is formed by the Yellow Sea, while its eastern border is defined by the Sea of Japan.

South Korea can be divided into four general regions: an eastern region of high mountain ranges and narrow coastal plains; a western region of broad coastal plains, river basins, and rolling hills; a southwestern region of mountains and valleys; and a southeastern region dominated by the broad basin of the Nakdong River.

South Korea is home to three terrestrial ecoregions: Central Korean deciduous forests, Manchurian mixed forests, and Southern Korea evergreen forests.

South Korea is the 22nd smallest country in Asia and ranked 109th in the world.

Korea's first kingdom was Old Chosun, which ruled the northwest and parts of China for more than 22 centuries.

In 1945, Korea was liberated from its occupation by Japan and, exactly three years later, on August 15, 1948, the Republic of Korea was officially established.

The National Liberation Day of South Korea is a holiday celebrated annually on 15 August.

Korean is the official language in both Southern and Northern Korea. Despite the difference in the dialects in the two countries, the two speakers can understand each other much easier.

한국어

조선말

Ethnicity of South Korea is predominantly Korean.

National founder of South Korea is Syngman Rhee.

National Motto of south Korea is "Devotion to the Welfare of Humanity".

Admiral Yi Sun-sin was a Korean admiral and military general famed for his victories against the Japanese navy during the Imjin war in the Joseon Dynasty.

National flag is "The flag of South Korea" also known as the Taegukgi.

The flag of Korea has three parts: a white rectangular background, a red and blue Taegeuk in its center, and four black trigrams, one in each corner.

In the flag the white color background represents peace and purity. The circle in the flag's center symbolizes balance in the universe. The red half represents positive cosmic forces, and the blue half represents the opposing negative cosmic forces. The trigrams represent movement and harmony as fundamental principles.

The national emblem is the "The National Coat of Arms of South Korea."

The National coat of arm of the
Republic of Korea consists of
the Taegeuk symbol present on
the South Korean national flag
surrounded by five flower petals
and a ribbon bearing the
inscription of the official Korean
name of the country.

The Taegeuk
represents
peace and
harmony.

The five petals all have meaning
and are related to South Korea's
national flower, the Hibiscus
syriacus, or Rose of Sharon.

The emblem was adopted on 10 December 1963.

National anthem of South Korea is Aegukga (Love Country Song).

The anthem's lyrics were written in 1896 by an unknown author and set to music by Ahn Eak-tai in 1936. It was officially adopted as the national anthem in 1948, when South Korea was founded.

National animal of South Korea is Korean tiger.

National flower of South Korea is Rose of Sharon / Hibiscus syriacus.

National bird of South Korea
is Korean magpie.

In Korea, the magpie is celebrated as a bird of great good fortune and provides prosperity and development. Korean children were also taught that when you lose a tooth, to throw it on the roof singing a song for the magpie. The bird will hear your song and bring you a new tooth.

National dish of South Korea is Kimchi.

Kimchi is a mixture of vegetables and various spices that is fermented. The dish gets its unique flavor from garlic, ginger, chili powder, red pepper, and sugar. Some fish sauce is also added to it. It is very popular and is served with almost all dishes.

Bandeja Paisa consists of rice, plantain, arepa (corn cakes), avocado, minced meat, chorizo, black sausage, and fried pork rind. There's also a fried egg thrown on top for good measure.

Breakfast is an important meal in Colombia. Lunch, however, is a serious affair. Most Colombians take a two-hour lunch break each day. For many Colombians, dinner is the least important meal of the day.

Kimjang is a traditional kimchi practice in South Korea. For several autumn days, families would give time to prepare the winter supply of kimchi. The annual Kimjang festival takes place in Gwangju, a city in the southwest region of the country.

The traditional Korean diet is centered around rice, vegetables, and meat dishes such as bulgogi and galbi.

South Korea is known for its popular cuisines like tteokbokki, Bulgogi, jjigae, Jajangmyeon and bibim nengmyun.

South Koreans are fond of sweet potatoes. Almost every possible dish has a sweet potato flavor. The list includes main courses, desserts, salads, bread, chips, latte, and even pizza.

National
fruit of
South Korea
is
Persimmons.

National drink of South
Korea is Makgeolli.

National tree of South Korea
is Korean red pine.

National colors of South Korea
are white, red, blue, and black.

National sports of South Korea is Taekwondo.

Taekwondo is a Korean martial arts involving punching and kicking techniques, with emphasis on head-height kicks, spinning jump kicks, and fast kicking techniques.

Taekwondo practitioners wear a uniform, known as a dobok. It is a combat sport and was developed during the 1940s and 1950s by Korean martial artists with experience in martial arts such as karate, Chinese martial arts, and indigenous Korean martial arts.

National dress of South Korea is Hanbok.

National instrument of South Korea is kayagum or gayageum

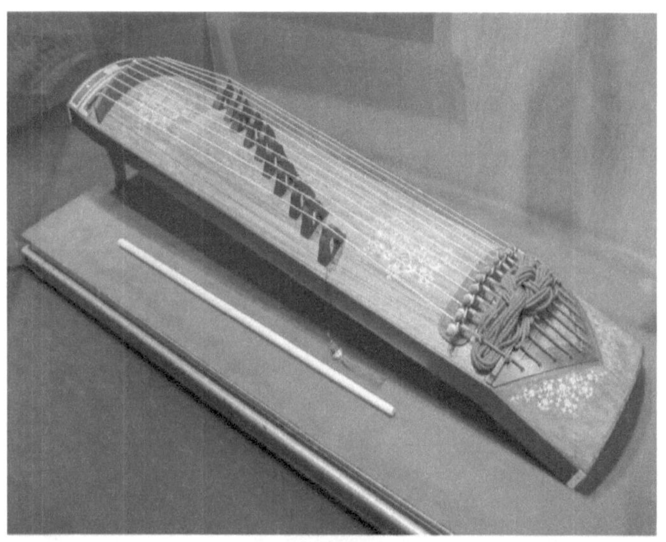

National dance of South Korea is Fan dance.

National monument of South Korea is Sungnyemun gate.

National airline of South Korea is Korean Air.

National currency of South
Korea is South Korean won.

Seoul officially known as the
Seoul Special City, is the capital
and largest metropolis of South
Korea.

Seoul is strategically located along the Han River and is surrounded by a mountainous and hilly landscape, with Bukhan Mountain located on the northern edge of the city.

The longest river in South Korea is the Naktong River

With major technology hubs centered in Gangnam and Digital Media City, the Seoul Capital Area is home to the headquarters of 15 Fortune Global 500 companies, including Samsung, LG, and Hyundai.

South Korea is home to the world's largest indoor theme park, Lotte World.

Lotte World consists of a large indoor theme park, an outdoor amusement park called "Magic Island", an artificial island (on a lake) linked by monorail, shopping malls, a luxury hotel, an observation tower, a Korean folk museum, sports facilities, and movie theaters.

The Cheomseongdae Observatory that was built at Gyeongju in the mid-600s, is the oldest surviving astronomical observatory in Asia.

Cheomseongdae was designated as the country's 31st national treasure on December 20, 1962.

Cheomseongdae influenced the construction of the Japanese Senseidai observatory in 675, and Duke Zhou's observatory in China in 723.

South Korea consists of over 4,000 islands.

South Korea is known for its beautiful natural landscapes, like the Jeju Island and the Seoraksan National Park.

Jeju island was formed by the eruption of an underwater volcano approximately 2 million years ago.

Jeju Island has a temperate climate which is moderate; even in winter, the temperature rarely falls below 0 °C (32 °F). Jeju is a popular holiday destination, and a sizable portion of the economy relies on tourism and related economic activity.

Jeju island contains a natural World Heritage Site, the Jeju Volcanic Island and Lava Tubes.

Seoraksan National Park is located on the east-central Korean peninsula, the reserve includes the Dinosaur Ridge, Injegun, Yanyanggun, and Sokchosi. It is popular with tourists and nature enthusiasts. It is home to many rare taxa of flora and fauna.

South Korea has 3 main rivers.
They are -Han River, Kŭm River,
and Naktong River. All three rivers
trace back to T'aebaek Mountains
where they flow between the
mountain ranges.

South Korea has 9 provinces.
They are Cheju, North Chŏlla,
South Chŏlla, North
Ch'ungch'ŏng, South
Ch'ungch'ŏng, Kangwŏn, Kyŏnggi,
North Kyŏngsang, and South
Kyŏngsang.

The Shinsegae Department Store in Centum City, Busan is the largest department store in the world.

According to the Organization for Economic Co-operation and Development (OECD), the South Korea has the highest estimated national IQ of any country in the world.

South Korea has a strong sense of
community, with many festivals and
events held throughout the year.

The Boryeong Mud Festival in
South Korea draws millions of
foreigners annually. For 10 days
of the event, mud massages,
mud marathons, mud wrestling
contests, and mud photo
contests are there to enjoy.

People in South Korea say 'kimchi' (instead of 'cheese') when they are taking photographs.

South Korea has one of the highest rates of plastic surgery in the world.

South Koreans celebrate the Harvest Moon Festival during which they travel to their hometowns and visit the graves of their ancestors and offer food.

South Koreans are remarkably healthy with only 3.2% of the population regarded as being overweight; they tie with Japan for having among the lowest levels of obesity in the world.

South Korean script is called Hangul. It consists of 14 consonants and 12 vowels, and it is relatively simple and uniform that helped to improve literacy.

Hangul, was created in the 15th century by King Sejong the Great.

Hangul Day or Korean alphabet day is observed on October 9 and has been a national holiday in South Korea since 1970.

Most alphabets around the world have mysterious, unknown origins. They slowly evolved from pictures into symbols that represent sounds. The Korean alphabet (Hangul or Hangeul) is different and unique among widely used alphabets. Rather than evolving, it was created deliberately.

Almost 82% of the total Korean population live in Urban area. The country's population is only 0.67% of the world's total population.

South Korea is one of the most densely populated countries in the world, with a population of over 51 million people in an area roughly the size of the state of Indiana.

South Koreans celebrate the new year twice. They celebrate the New Year at the start of the solar calendar (January 1), and once more on the first day of the year on the lunar calendar.

It is recorded that Kilnam
Chon played a major role in the
introduction of the Internet
to South Korea. The first Internet
message sent from South
Korea to the world was done by
Hyunje Park in 1990.

The government established policies and programs that facilitated the rapid expansion and use of broadband. The country has 97.6% of the population owning a smartphone, which is the highest in the world.

South Korea has a strong film industry, known as "Hallyuwood," which produces popular dramas and films that are popular throughout Asia.

The country is also known for its K-pop music, with bands such as BTS and BLACKPINK achieving worldwide fame.

K- Pop includes styles and genres from around the world on top of its traditional Korean music roots.

Black pink is a K-Pop girl group formed by YG Entertainment and the biggest K-pop girl band in the world.

South Korea has a high literacy rate of 97.9%.

The country has a life expectancy of 83 years, one of the highest in the world.

South Korea has a strong education system, with students typically attending school from the age of six to 18.

The country has several top-ranked universities, including Seoul National University and Korea University

Seoul National University (SNU) was founded on August 27, 1946, by merging ten institutions of higher education around the Seoul area.

The university comprises sixteen colleges, one graduate school and nine professional schools.

SNU is widely considered to be the most prestigious university in South Korea, and 31st most innovative institution in the world.

Korea University (KU) is a private research university in Seoul which is established in 1905. The university is included as one of the SKY Universities, a popular acronym referring to Korea's three most prestigious universities.

South Korea has a strong fashion industry and is known for its street fashion and designer clothing.

 K-Fashion or K-Style is getting popularity all over the world and many young people are consuming K-fashion and K-beauty as K-pop and K-dramas gain popularity.

South Korea has a strong focus on technology and innovation, with many companies investing heavily in research and development.

South Korea has a high standard of living and is considered one of the most developed countries in Asia.

Korean people are known for their intelligence and work ethic. The country has one of the highest average annual work hours.

Minors under the age of 18 are not allowed to work unless they have written permission from their parents or guardians.

The country has a highly developed transportation infrastructure, including high-speed trains and a subway system.

South Korea is one of the world's leading producers of steel.

Incheon International Airport is the primary airport serving the Seoul Capital Area and one of the largest and busiest airports in the world.

The airport has been rated by Skytrax as the fourth-best airport in the world. Skytrax also has rated the airport as the world's best international transit airport and one of the world's cleanest airports.

South Korea is home to many traditional temples and palaces, including Gyeongbokgung Palace and Bulguksa Temple.

Gyeongbokgung was originally constructed in 1394 by King Taejo, the first king and the founder of the Joseon dynasty.

Gyeongbokgung served as the home of Kings of the Joseon dynasty, the Kings' households, as well as the government of Joseon.

The world's first commercially available MP3 player, the MPMan, was launched by SaeHan Information Systems in 1997.

Developed by a team at Korea Institute of Science and Technology and introduced in March 2005, MAHRU (originally known as NBH-1) is the first network-based humanoid robot in the world.

Introduced in 2005, Albert HUBO is the world's first walking humanoid robot with an android head. It was a collaboration between Hanson Robotics and KAIST.

In 2000, LG
Electronics introduced the
world's first digital
refrigerator called
the Internet Digital DIOS.

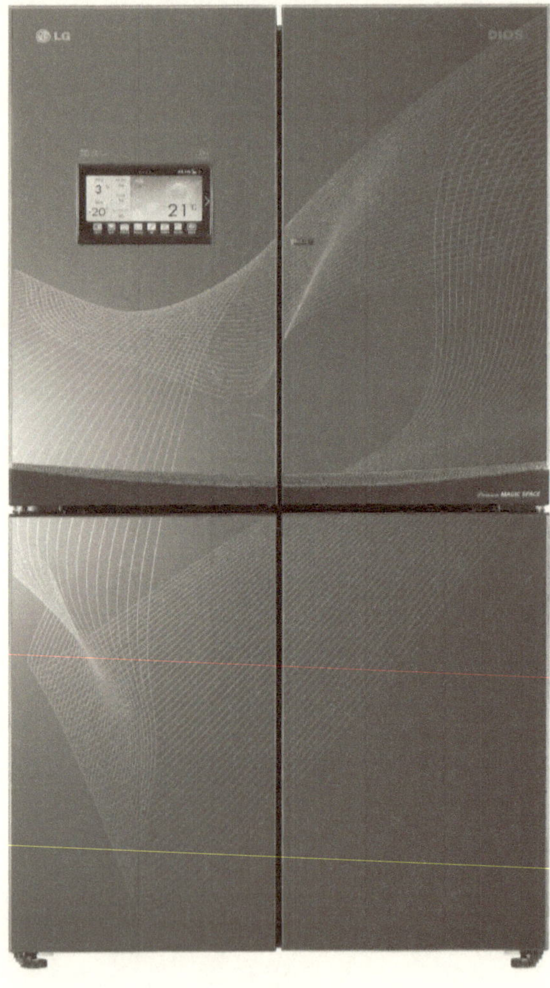

Hongsoo Choi's research team has developed the world's first ciliary microrobots, that can move and function like single cells.

South Korea's Method-2 is the world's first manned bipedal robot introduced to the World.

Please check this out:

Our other best-selling books for kids are-

Ukraine: Interesting & Amazing Facts That Everyone Should Know

Germany: Interesting & Amazing Facts That Everyone Should Know

Switzerland: Interesting & Amazing Facts That Everyone Should Know

New Zealand: Interesting & Amazing Facts That Everyone Should Know

Brazil: Interesting & Amazing Facts That Everyone Should Know

Argentina: Interesting & Amazing Facts That Everyone Should Know

Chile: Interesting & Amazing Facts That Everyone Should Know

Denmark Interesting & Amazing Facts That Everyone Should Know

All About **Canada**: Interesting & Amazing Facts That Everyone Should Know

All About **Australia**: Interesting & Amazing Facts That Everyone Should Know

All About **Italy**: Interesting & Amazing Facts That Everyone Should Know

Please check this out:
Our other best-selling books for kids are-
All About **France**: Interesting & Amazing Facts That
Everyone Should Know
All About **Japan:** Interesting & Amazing Facts That
Everyone Should Know
Know About Whales: Interesting & Amazing Facts That
Everyone Should Know
Know About Dinosaurs: Interesting & Amazing Facts That
Everyone Should Know
Know About Kangaroos: Interesting & Amazing Facts That
Everyone Should Know
Know About Penguins: Interesting & Amazing Facts That
Everyone Should Know
Know About Dolphins :100 Interesting & Amazing Facts That Everyone Should Know
Know About Elephant: Interesting & Amazing Facts That
Everyone Should Know

Please check this out:

Our other best-selling books for kids are-

100 Amazing Quiz Q & A About Penguin: Never Known Before Penguin Facts

Most Popular Animal Quiz book for Kids: 100 amazing animal facts

Quiz Book for Kids: Science, History, Geography, Biology, Computer & Information Technology

English Grammar for Kids: Most Easy Way to learn English Grammar

Solar System & Space Science- Quiz for Kids: What You Know About Solar System

English Grammar Practice Book for elementary kids: 1000+ Practice Questions with Answers